IMAGES
of England

CLACTON-
ON-SEA

Welcome to Clacton! This picture of Nora Steadman was taken by the Council publicity chief, Harry Thompson, in the early 1950s. Nora's picture was used time and time again against different backgrounds to advertise the charms of Clacton in both local guides and in the national press. She was born in Burrsville and became Carnival Queen in 1951. It was said that she had a 'sunshine personality and was a great asset to the town. She just sparkled.' Nora later married British featherweight boxing champion, Bobby Neill.

IMAGES
of England

CLACTON-
ON-SEA

Compiled by
Norman Jacobs

TEMPUS

First published 2000
Copyright © Norman Jacobs, 2000

Tempus Publishing Limited
The Mill, Brimscombe Port,
Stroud, Gloucestershire, GL5 2QG

ISBN 0 7524 1857 2

Typesetting and origination by
Tempus Publishing Limited
Printed in Great Britain by
Midway Clark Printing, Wiltshire

A lively beach scene from the 1950s, showing the *Nemo II* pleasure boat, the Punch & Judy stand, the Steel Stella roller coaster and the crowds who flocked to Clacton at that time.

Contents

This Scouts race, held around 1907, was won by O. Ward, who received a silver cup for his efforts. The race was held on Easter Monday in conjunction with Clacton Athletic Club and the course was from outside the Palace to Anglefield. The event was witnessed by a large holiday crowd and the judges were Dr Slimon and Mrs D.H. Howard.

Introduction

Much has already been written about how Clacton-on-Sea came to be founded. How Peter Bruff, Victorian engineer and entrepreneur extraordinaire, bought up the land in 1865 with the specific purpose of turning it into a seaside resort; and how, with the backing of William Parry Jackson and the Woolwich Steam Packet Company and beginning with the Pier in 1871 followed by the Royal Hotel in 1872, his idea gradually came to fruition and Clacton-on-Sea came to be one of the leading seaside resorts in the country.

Of course, Bruff was lucky in the fact that Clacton is in one of the sunniest and driest regions of Great Britain. It's not known as the Sunshine Coast or Sunny Clacton for nothing! So, before coming to the photographs, I thought it would be worth looking at an excerpt from a 1920 guide book to Clacton which spelled out this good fortune in more detail:

'To large numbers of people the words "Sunny Clacton" bring happy recollections of delightful holidays in one of the healthiest towns in England. As soon as the traveller leaves the Great Eastern Railway station he realises the vast difference between the air of London and the health-giving properties of the ozone-laden atmosphere of this popular and up-to-date Health Resort. Those who associate the East Coast with piercing winds are surprised to find that they must alter their views after visiting Clacton-on-Sea.'

This latter statement may come as a bit of a surprise to those of us who live here, but if that's what the book says it must be right! I was talking to local journalist Ernest Hall recently. In the 1950s Ernest worked for Clacton Urban District Council as a part-time weatherman. He told me that in the interests of the holiday industry they always had to make the best of the weather. If the forecast was a good one they would stress that it was *continuing* fine, warm and sunny. That made day trippers wish they were staying for a week. When the weather wasn't all that could be hoped for, they had to choose their words carefully. 'Dull' was a word that was never used. Clacton might occasionally be cloudy, but never dull. The wind was another matter. 'Yes', he said to me, 'we all knew perfectly well that many a spring day has been marred by a bitter north-east wind blowing all the way from Murmansk, but we preferred to think of this phenomenon as bracing!'

In July 1956 there were gale-force winds in which trees were uprooted, boats were sunk and the Cresta Run on the Pier was blown in to the sea. If you'd had the courage and resolution to fight your way across Pier Gap to the weather report notice board, and had wiped the salt spray off the glass front, you would have read 'Sunny periods, risk of showers, breezy.'

However, I digress. Back to the 1920 guide book: 'It is beyond question that Clacton has the largest amount of sunshine of any seaside place within easy reach of London and that rainfall is literally the smallest in England.... The late Dr Slimon has said that "the bracing air – charged with ozone – has a most beneficial influence upon all affections of the upper air passages and bronchial diseases." Dr P. Coleman has extolled the virtues of Clacton-on-Sea as a place almost immune from pneumonia, Bright's Disease and rheumatic fever, and attributes this fact to the smallness of the rainfall, large amounts of sunshine and equability of temperature. Thus we have it established on medical evidence that the porous nature of the soil, the small rainfall, the abundance of sunshine and the position on the coast combine together to make Clacton an ideal health resort.' (It makes you wonder how Dr Slimon ever became the *late* Dr Slimon....)

With all that going for Clacton, how could Bruff have failed in his business venture? Well, of course, he couldn't and he didn't. Bruff's vision, as we all know, became a reality, and particularly during the inter-war years and in the 1950s, Clacton-on-Sea became one of the leading seaside resorts in the country. But it wasn't just the weather. Clacton Urban District Council was always a very go-ahead council, prepared to invest in Clacton's future – for many years it also provided all the gas, water and electricity for Clacton. So were local business families, such as the Harmans, the Foysters, the Kingsmans, the Anselmis, the Pennells, the Quicks and many others.

At one end of the beach, the Pier, affectionately known as No. 1 North Sea, was providing all types of entertainments and amusements, from theatres to penny arcades, from dodgems to dance halls and from a roller coaster to a swimming pool. At the other end, Butlin's was allowing day visitors into its pleasure park, its indoor games rooms and its elegant Viennese Ballroom. In between there was the roller skating rink, donkey rides or, if you preferred, room for quiet contemplation in the sunken gardens. In 1939, Clacton had six cinemas and ten theatres operating simultaneously.

This book is in many ways a tribute to the work of all the people and organizations who helped turn a windy desolate strip of land by the North Sea in to the 'Sun and fun showbizzy champagne sea and air resort' of Clacton-on-Sea.

I have many people to thank for their help in compiling this book. In particular I should like to thank Peter Underhay, Ken Brown, Chris Connolly, Linda Oliver, Linda Fitch, Roger Kennell, George Hardwick, Reg Young, Tendring District Council and the Clacton and District Local History Society either for the loan of photographs or for valuable information. I would also like to thank David Mantripp for keeping his shop open long enough to copy some of the photographs for me. And last, but not least, I would like to thank my own family for the support they have given me: my mum, for providing food and drink while I was slaving away over a hot computer; my son Tom for allowing me to use his computer in the first place; my wife, Linda, for agreeing to forego the dining room table for several months while I kept laying out photographs in many and varied combinations; and my other son, Robert for... for being Robert.

I should like to dedicate this book to the memory of my dear old dad, who first introduced me to Clacton and Butlin's all those years ago and who died just as I started the preparation for this book.

One
Peter Bruff's Brainchild

The centre of Sunny Clacton is seen here between the wars when it was at its height as a seaside resort. Grimwade & Clarke, 'high-class outfitters', closed in 1983 after a span of some eighty years at the heart of Clacton, to be replaced by a McDonald's restaurant.

When this photograph was taken in 1872 this is practically all there was of Clacton-on-Sea: the Pier and the Royal Hotel sitting alone on the cliff top.

Before 1871, Clacton Beach, as it was known, boasted just a few coastguard cottages and farm buildings and three Martello towers, built in the early nineteenth century to guard against invasion by Napoleon. This is the tower at the foot of Tower Road, in use for much of this century as a coastguard look-out.

CLACTON-ON-SEA.

The rapidly rising and favourite Seaside Resort, the nearest Seaside Town to London on the East Coast, 95 minutes by rail from Liverpool Street, Southern Aspect, Bracing Climate, Gravel Soil, Good Drainage, Fine Pier, Pavilion, and Promenades, Steamboat communication with London, Walton-on-Naze, Harwich, Ipswich, and Yarmouth daily, Golf Club, Fast Train Service, Cheap Season and Residential Tickets.

Important Sale of Freehold Building Land and Marine Residences.

Particulars, Plans and Conditions of Sale

32 Plots of Valuable Freehold
BUILDING LAND,

Ripe for immediate Building, and very suitable for the erection of

Private Residences, Bungalows, Shops, and Business Premises,

And having important frontages to the Marine Parade, Albert Road, Alton Road, Carnarvon Road, Granville Road, Holland Road, High Street, Hubert Road, Lancaster Gardens, North Road, Oliver's Road, St. Osyth Road, Thoroughgood Road, Vista Road, Wellesley Road, etc., and including

5 VALUABLE SHOP PLOTS IN HIGH STREET,

Good for the erection of Business Premises, for which there is a great demand;

8 Capital Plots in St. Osyth Road, ripe for the erection of small Villa Properties; and a

CHOICE AND VALUABLE FREEHOLD BUILDING PLOT,

Immediately facing the Sea; also the following desirable **Freehold**

MARINE RESIDENCES.

"EATON & PORTLAND HOUSES," Marine Parade.—Two splendidly situate residences, immediately facing the sea, and bound to rapidly increase in value.
"BELMONT, GLENCOTE, STAMFORD & LOTHAIR HOUSES," Station Road. Four very desirable marine residences, well fitted and finished, and situate in main road leading from station to sea.
"SUNSHINE & ELLY LODGES," Wellesley Road. Two newly erected detached villas, standing in own grounds, good position for rail and sea. Sold with possession.
"CLARENCE & YORK VILLAS," St. Paul's Road. Two newly erected semi-detached villas, situate near the sea. Sold with possession.
"Nos. 1 to 4 LYDFORD VILLAS," Wellesley Road. Four newly erected villas, situate in good letting part, and of a class and size for which there is a capital demand. Sold with possession.
"No. 1 ALBION VILLAS," Fairfield Road. Very compact residence, well situate for sea and rail. Sold with possession. The whole Properties being of the estimated

RENTAL VALUE OF £700 PER ANN.

To be Sold by Auction by

Edwin J. Gilders

AT THE ROYAL HOTEL, CLACTON-ON-SEA,
ON THURSDAY, AUGUST 17th, 1899,
At 3.30 for 4 o'clock precisely.

☞ The greater portion of the Purchase-Money for the properties can remain on mortgage (if desired) and in most cases payments for the plots of land by instalments can be arranged.

Particulars, Plans and Conditions of Sale may be obtained from the principal Hotels; from Messrs. CHAMBERLAYNE and SHORT, Solicitors, Donington House, Norfolk Street, Strand, and Clacton-on-Sea; Messrs. G. READER & Co., Solicitors, 1 Chapel Place, Poultry, E.C.; C. H. T. MARSHALL, Esq., Solicitor, Colchester; Messrs. SAVERY & STEVENS, Solicitors, 6 Fen Court, Fenchurch Street, E.C.; Messrs. WITTEY & DENTON, Solicitors, Colchester; and from the Auctioneer's Offices:—
STATION ROAD, CLACTON-ON-SEA, and 10, UNION COURT, LONDON, E.C.

The Clacton-on-Sea Graphic Printing and Publishing Company.

As a new town, much building took place during the nineteenth century and many plots of land were sold off at auction as building land. This is the notice for one such auction held by Edwin J. Gilders at the Royal Hotel in 1899. Edwin J. Gilders is still today very much a part of Clacton's estate agent scene.

On the left corner of this view looking up Rosemary Road in around 1890 is Walbrook House, home of the combined offices of the Land, the Gas and Water, the Pier and the Steamboat companies. This corner later became known as Wagstaff's Corner, by which name it is still known today. Further along the road is the studio of Paul Fries, photographer.

This is Rosemary Road East in the 1930s, with the Co-op, opened just after the First World War, on the left and the Eastern National bus station on the right.

This photograph was taken around 1890 in the days when Pier Gap was lined by shops. These were swept away in 1914 when Clacton Council decided to implement a 'general beautifying programme' and replaced the shops with gardens and the Venetian Bridge.

A view of Pier Gap in 1914, shortly after the opening ceremony – as evidenced by all the flags. At the opening ceremony the Mayor of West Ham congratulated the Council on 'replacing the eel-pie shops... with beautiful flower beds and the bridge.'

The top of Pier Gap, *c.* 1890. The picture also shows the children who offered goat-cart rides for 2d a time. The carts were licensed by Clacton Council, but in 1893 they decided not to issue licenses to children under eleven and the goat cart rides finished shortly afterwards.

On the right of this busy Edwardian scene at the junction of Pier Avenue and Marine Parade is the Royal Hotel. Just outside the Royal is a policeman who was probably on traffic duty, although his services don't seem to be much in demand.

By the time of this photograph of the same corner taken in the late '20s, the traffic policeman had been given his own box! This was apparently a dangerous occupation as on a number of occasions cars came careering round the corner and crashed into the box. There are now traffic lights on this corner.

The large building on the left of this 1920s view of Pier Avenue was the old Public Hall, built by the town's pioneers in 1877. Much of the building was later occupied by Lewellen's ironmonger's. On the right is the booking office for National Coaches, with boards outside advertising half-day and day trips to local places of interest.

Electric Parade was opened on 23 July 1901 and was so-called because it was the first street in Clacton to have electric lighting. This was a private supply paid for and operated by the shopkeepers themselves. It wasn't until 1906 that the Council itself established an electricity works in the town.

The name Electric Parade continued until about 1959, the time of this photograph, when it fell into disuse and the street became a continuation of Pier Avenue.

On the right of this 1950s view looking up Electric Parade from the junction with Station Road is the elm tree, still at the centre of Clacton today and the town's last reminder of its fairly recent rural past.

Strangely enough, although the right-hand side of the road was known as Electric Parade, the left hand side was always part of Pier Avenue, here seen in around 1905. In the background is the Castle Restaurant, opened in 1901.

63436　PIER AVENUE, CLACTON-ON-SEA.

The top end of Pier Avenue, *c.* 1960. The Milk Bar is on the extreme right. Gilders Brothers & Brown first moved into Electric Parade from Rosemary Road as a dairy just after the First World War, later becoming a snack bar trading first as Gilders & Brown Snack Bar and finally as the Milk Bar. It closed in 1969.

18

The London & County Bank shown on the left of this Edwardian view of Station Road at its junction with Pier Avenue was designed by local architect T.H. Baker and opened in 1899. After several mergers it became the NatWest, by which name it is still known today. T.H. Baker was also the architect for Christ Church and St Osyth Road School.

In this late 1930s view from the same junction, looking the other way up the tree-lined Station Road, it is evident that the Town Clock was a prominent feature of Clacton before the war.

This view of the Station Road, Rosemary Road and High Street corner from around 1891 shows the empty plots of land that were shortly to become the Town Hall and the Arcade Buildings. It is possible the boards facing the road were advertising the sale of the land.

The shop on the corner of this 1891 view looking down Station Road was then known as Bayswater House and was owned by Mrs Phillips, a wardrobe dealer. It was on this site that the farm, Sea Side House Farm, which had originally owned the land that was to become Clacton-on-Sea, stood.

By 1904, the date of this photograph, Frederick Wagstaff had become firmly established in his corner as a tobacconist and the Town Hall had been built. The buildings comprised a bank on the ground floor, council offices upstairs and a theatre, the Operetta House, to the rear. The Town Hall had opened in April 1894 to house the Local Board of Health offices, but all Local Boards of Health were dissolved at the end of 1894 and their place taken by urban or rural district councils and so on 9 January 1895 the Great Clacton Urban District Council held its first meeting in these offices. The 'Great' was dropped within six months and the council vacated the premises in 1923.

This is the corner of Rosemary Road and Pier Avenue some time between 1881, when the water tower was built, and 1887, when a schoolroom was added to the Wesleyan church. The water tower was acquired by the Council in 1899 when it bought the Gas & Water Co. and brought it under council ownership. It was 101 feet high and held 30,000 gallons of water. In 1962 the Council handed over the water supply to the Tendring Hundred Waterworks Co., who closed the tower down in 1968 and demolished it shortly thereafter.

CLACTON-ON-SEA. — *Wesleyan Church.* —LL.

The Wesleyan church, later called Trinity church, was opened on 14 August 1877 and could accommodate 500 people. At that time the total population of Clacton was less than 500! The schoolroom to the rear, just visible in this Edwardian view of the church, was opened in 1887 and within one year had 225 children on its register.

By the time of this photograph, in the 1950s, Trinity church was no longer in a rural setting, but was now at the centre of a busy, built-up junction. It still today caters for the town's Methodist congregation and is one of the oldest buildings still standing in the centre of Clacton-on-Sea.

Ever since Peter Bruff first built the pier in 1871, Clacton-on-Sea has continued to expand steadily with big spurts of growth in the 1920s and again after the Second World War. Typical of the new post-war roads is this part of Douglas Road near the junction with Cloes Lane, photographed here on 15 April 1959.

Now at the centre of an industrial estate, it is hard to imagine that Oxford Road ever looked like this. Yet as late as the 1960s Clacton Guide Books were reproducing similar views of Oxford Road to this one, taken in 1959, with captions such as 'A rural retreat near Clacton.'

Two

The Village of Clacc's People

While all the hectic building was going on in the new town of Clacton-on-Sea, the old village of Great Clacton continued on its peaceful way. This picture from the 1950s shows how little it had changed for two or three centuries, apart perhaps for the advertisement for the West Cliff Theatre on the wall.

St Osyth Main Road (now St John's Road) during the Edwardian period showing E. Culham & Son, wine, spirit and beer merchants, occupying the building known as St John's House. This was built in the early nineteenth century and at one time was home to Henry Finer, first chairman of Clacton Urban District Council and owner of the first grocery shop in Clacton-on-Sea.

The Queen's Head, seen here between the wars, was built around 1600 but did not become an inn until seventy years later. The large bow-fronted extension was added during the Napoleonic period when the locally stationed soldiers made the landlord of the Queen's Head a rich man! At the back of the Queen's Head was one of the village smithies.

The Ship Inn, photographed here in the early years of the twentieth century, dates back to around 1500, and is possibly the second oldest building still standing in Clacton (after St John's church). Originally a yeoman's cottage, it became an inn in the early eighteenth century and was bought by John Cobbold in 1800.

The Old Mill, Clacton-on-Sea.

Great Clacton's windmill, photographed shortly before its demolition in 1918. This post-mill had long since ceased to be a working mill, having been overtaken by new technology when, in 1867, Mr Charles Beckwith, its owner, built a steam mill nearby. Its memory lives on in the name of Windmill Park, which is where it was situated.

Sewell & Sweeting farmers, of Elm Farm, Bocking's Elm, owned this fine horse and cart photographed here in the 1930s.

In 1932, Clacton-on-Sea began to expand beyond the old village of Great Clacton when William Renshaw built up the Burrsville Park Estate, starting with The Drive. By the start of the Second World War, some 250 houses had been built, mostly bungalows for retired people. This is a view of the corner of Burrs Road and Gorse Lane in 1940.

Three
The Village of Stedman's People

Labour MP George Lansbury greets Miss Jaywick, Gladys Pritchard, at the Jaywick Sands Freeholders' Association Gala in August 1934.

Clacton Urban District Council Election

MONDAY, AUGUST 15th, 1938

Polling Station:
St. Osyth Road School, Clacton-on-Sea

Vote——STEDMAN

In 1928 Frank Christopher Stedman bought up a large area to the west of Clacton known as Jaywick and set about turning it into a holiday resort called Jaywick Sands. Right from the beginning he encountered much opposition from Clacton Council, whose members thought the area highly unsuitable for building on due to its propensity to flooding. In 1938, in order to try to get a voice on the Council, his son Reginald stood for election. His bid was unsuccessful and the Stedmans' clash with officialdom continued unabated.

In spite of these problems, however, Jaywick Sands did develop into a lively seaside resort and here we see a visit from the *Daily Herald* publicity van in August 1937.

'For the health and happiness of the children, every morning at 11 a.m. drill and physical exercises will be held on the Café Green.' These classes were organized by Peter Marsh, otherwise known as 'Uncle Peter'. Here he is seen in front of the children in a photograph taken in 1935.

Another 1935 photograph, this time of holidaymakers enjoying themselves on Jaywick's sandy beach.

J 138   Hillman Avenue, Jaywick Sands.

Jaywick was divided into four areas: Brooklands, Grasslands, Old Town and the Tudor Estate. This is Brooklands, in which all the streets were named after popular makes of motor car, such as this one, Hillman Avenue, seen in 1934.

In the centre of a busy Broadway pictured in July 1956 is Dot's. Originally Dot's Tuck Shop, it has been involved in Jaywick from its beginnings right up to the present day.

The Café Morocco, seen here in the 1930s, was built in 1934 as a dance hall and called the Morocco Café Ballroom. After the war it became known as the 'Nightspot on Broadway'. In 1980 it became a late-night disco called the 'Metro Club' and in 1984 it became the Morocco Social Club. It closed down in 1987 and was demolished in 1991.

Clacton Council's view of the unsuitability of Jaywick for building on seemed to be confirmed in 1936 when the area was flooded. This is Brooklands Gardens looking west on 2 December 1936.

Far worse was to come in 1953, when the full fury of the East Coast floods struck Jaywick on the night of 31 January/1 February. This disaster caused the deaths of thirty-five people as well as untold destruction to property.

The police had a busy night that night. This police car, still covered with hay from haystacks which had been washed away from Wigborough Farm, travelled around 3,000 miles in the course of its rescue mission.

The 1953 floods had been foreseen by Adrian Wolfe, chairman of the Freeholders' Association. At a special meeting in 1950 he promised members he would ensure a new sea wall was built before the end of the year. True to his word, work finished on the new sea wall on the very last day of 1950 and was officially opened on 18 May 1951. This is the start of the wall in early 1950.

Four

From Little Holland to Holland-on-Sea

In the early 1920s, when this photograph was taken, Holland-on-Sea was still known as Little Holland. However, as can be seen by the caption, the 'on-Sea' bit was just beginning to creep into the name. This view of King's Avenue looking across Holland Road shows F.W. Hazleton's greengrocer's shop on the left next to Milbourne's King's Cliff stores and post office.

Little Holland Church and Main Road.

This view, also taken in the 1920s, shows the original corrugated iron church of St Bartholomew's, which was dedicated in 1903. It was replaced in 1929 by a second church, which was itself replaced in 1971 by the present church. Further along the road is the Princess Helena public house on the site of what is now the Roaring Donkey.

Kings Cliff Hotel & Cliffs. Holland-on-Sea. 266

By the end of the 1930s (this view dates from *c.* 1937), Holland-on-Sea was becoming popular as a small seaside resort. This area of beach was developed by Walter Johnson, whose orange and white striped beach hut can be seen at the foot of the cliffs. Further along the beach are the foundations for one of several pavilions built along the beach.

38

Strictly speaking, this 1920s view of the beach is in Clacton, but is looking up towards Holland-on-Sea. As can be seen, this area of the beach was already becoming very popular with holidaymakers.

The same stretch of beach after development at about the time of the Second World War. Note the sewage outfall in the distance.

The Queen's Hall at the bottom of King's Avenue, opened in 1935 and seen here in the 1950s, was a popular local theatre putting on many first-class shows.

The interior of the Queen's Hall theatre, again in the 1950s. It was demolished in 1972 to make way for the block of flats which now occupies the site.

The King's Cliff Hotel and cliff path, c. 1938. This photograph provides evidence of Holland's recent rural past, as the plough lines can still be seen in the grass.

Even more evidence of Holland's rural past can be seen in this photograph of Bournemouth Road being laid out in 1939.

The Holland-on-Sea Rifle Club was opened on 29 August 1934 by Cllr H.F. Bartlett. The president, Mrs L.L. Griggs, is seen speaking at the opening ceremony.

Five

Support Your Local Businesses

M. Appleby's Dining Rooms in Pier Avenue, seen here in the 1880s, were described in the 1888 *Line's Directory* for Clacton as the 'People's Café – Parties catered for'. It had disappeared by the 1902 Directory.

The Clacton Tea Table, seen here around 1890, was owned by Henry Foyster, who owned two other businesses in Clacton, a shop and a restaurant. This shop in Rosemary Road, next to where the Indoor Market is today, seems to have been both.

Fred Walker's music shop, seen here in the 1920s, moved to Station Road from Rosemary Road just before the First World War. It was located two doors away from Wagstaff's Corner. In its early days it sold musical instruments, but by the time of its closure in the 1930s it was selling mostly records and sheet music.

This cheque dated 7 November 1891 was drawn on Mills Bawtree Dawney Curzon & Co.'s Bank by Abraham Quick & Co. The bank opened as Mills Errington Bawtree & Co. in Colne Road in 1882. On 15 December 1891 a telegram arrived from their head office saying the bank had failed and that the branch was to suspend all business immediately. It is said that the postmaster, Mr S.G. Wallis, rushed round to the bank and withdrew all his savings before delivering the fateful telegram!

W.H. Smith & Son's first shop in Clacton, photographed here around 1902, was on the opposite side of Pier Avenue to where it is now. It moved to its present position in 1927, when the post office, which had occupied the site, moved to the High Street.

Abraham Quick and Co. Ltd published the *Clacton News* and its successor the *East Essex Gazette* for around seventy-five years. This is the staff outside its first office in Station Road, where visitors could be 'conducted over the premises on presentation of a card', in 1890. Abraham Quick himself is seated fourth from the right on the front row.

At about the time of the First World War, Quick's offices were moved to Jackson Road. In this picture taken in 1954 they are seen sandwiched between Goldsmith's Car Hire Service and Grey Green Coaches.

The Corner House Café on the corner of Pier Avenue and Marine Parade, seen here in the 1920s, was a very popular eating place throughout the inter-war and immediate post-war years.

The Grosvenor Corner House café was situated on the corner of Colne Road and Pallister Road next to the Comrades Club. Its owner was Michael Gabri. It is seen here in the late 1930s.

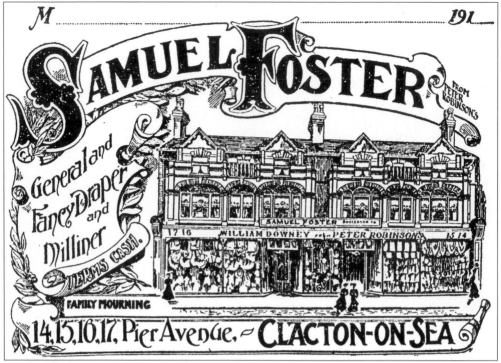

During the late Victorian and Edwardian period many of the local businesses had very elaborate letter headings. This is Samuel Foster's, *c.* 1910. Samuel Foster was a General & Fancy Draper and Milliner who occupied the premises next to Grimwade and Clarke in Pier Avenue for many years.

Manager Billy Buxton is seen here with the staff of the International Stores during the Edwardian period. There were two International Stores in Clacton, one in Station Road, the other in Pier Avenue. The latter was destroyed in the Lewellen's fire of 1939.

Before the Little Clacton Safeway store was built the land belonged to the Horsefall family who kept a poultry farm on the site. This is a view of the farm in the early 1930s. The car is a Bullnose Morris Cowley which was bought by the farmer for £12 and used mainly for transporting chicken feed around the farm.

Adjacent to the poultry farm was Everitt's Sweet Pea Nurseries, which started in 1928 when Ruaton Gardens moved away from the site. As well as sweet peas, they specialized in fresh cut flowers, tomatoes and cucumbers. Everitt's closed in 1972 when the land was sold to Highfield's Holiday Park.

In the early days of the resort many schools and colleges were established, as the bracing sea air was felt to be an aid to education. The College, seen here shortly after its foundation in 1881, was one such boys' school. About ten years later it was converted into the Waverley Hotel.

The Waverley is still today one of the leading hotels in Clacton. This is a view of the buffet during the 1950s, with its owner, Leslie Price, behind the bar. Leslie later became the Council's Leisure Manager and Secretary to the West Cliff Theatre Trust.

The Oulton Hall was the last major hotel to be built in Clacton, opening in the mid-1930s. This view was taken in 1936. It was a temperance hotel and had the slogan 'Where holidays are jolidays'. It was closed in 1966 and became part of the St Osyth Teacher Training College until it was sold in the 1980s and converted in to a block of flats.

During the 1950s and more particularly the 1960s the nature of holidays in Clacton changed to do-it-yourself type holidays in flats and caravan parks. Highfield's, one of the biggest caravan parks, is seen here shortly after it opened in the late 1960s.

F.H. & W.G. French had an ironmongery shop in Old Road from just after the First World War until the 1950s. This is an exhibition of their wares probably at the Tendring Show in 1928. Frank French is second from the right, while Geoffrey, his son, is second from the left.

Before Marks & Spencer came to Clacton, the site was occupied by Arthur Westwood of Westwood's Motors, later Westwood and Clark. This is a view of the shop just after they had closed down and before Marks & Spencer moved in, the date being 19 January 1934.

Shortly after moving in, Marks & Spencer expanded the shop and created an entrance at the rear on to West Avenue. This photograph, taken in 1935, shows the back entrance being widened.

This is a drawing of Hodgson & Co. Ltd, Builders' Merchants, some time in the late 1940s or early '50s. Hodgson occupied the corner of High Street and Beach Road for some fifty years from before the First World War until the 1960s.

Cook & Eaves in Pier Avenue (Electric Parade), seen here at 11.30 a.m. on Saturday 18 July 1959 (if only everyone could date their photographs so precisely!), started life as Eaves in Pier Gap and moved to Electric Parade in 1914 after the Pier Gap shops were demolished. Next door to Cook & Eaves is MacFisheries. Many Clactonians will still remember their genial manager of this period, Mr John 'Buff' Dove.

Six

Come to Sunny Clacton!

As a seaside resort, Clacton has always relied on publicizing its virtues to entice the visitors. This was how it was done in the 1930s. But things did improve...

In February 1952, Clacton Council appointed the twenty-six-year-old Harry Thompson to be its new Assistant Entertainment and Publicity Manager. By April of that year, Harry had already completed two publicity tours to places such as Birmingham, Coventry, Leicester, Nottingham, London, Oxford and Reading. Harry bubbled over with new ideas of how to publicize the town and, by the end of the year, the traders in Southend were complaining that Clacton was taking all their trade away from them. Harry is on the left of this photograph receiving the prize for the best float in the Hendon Carnival of 1953 from Cllr A.V. Sully, Mayor of Hendon.

Harry spared no expense in his organization of the float for the Hendon Carnival, seen above. The three 'bathing beauties' on the float were Miss Great Britain, Miss Bikini of the World and Miss English Rose. 25,000 people attended the Hendon Carnival. The following year the same float won first prize in the Edmonton Carnival.

Throughout the 1950s, during the winter months, Harry arranged for a converted coach to tour the country, showing the publicity film *Back to the Sun*. The coach was provided by Premier Travel, the only coach company to provide a direct service from Clacton to the Midlands and the North.

Northern winters were a bit hard on some of the girls Harry took along to support the publicity coach! But it gained results as in 1954 the *Birmingham Evening Post*, readership 200,000, published a three-column picture on its front page of a girl in a swimsuit walking through the streets in a blizzard saying 'Sunny Clacton'.

Harry also organized major events in the towns he visited, such as The Holiday Girl Contest for which heats were held all over the country with the winners competing in the final in Clacton during the summer. This is another similar event, the 'Miss Clacton on Ice' in 1954, held in Birmingham.

Harry also had a keen eye for the publicity photograph. This is one of his from the 1950s, taken on the East Beach just below the Band Pavilion.

Another from 1958, combining the publicity shot, looking down on the Pier, with the publicity created through that year's Holiday Girl competition. Harry Thompson continued his work for Clacton Urban District Council and later Tendring District Council for some thirty years before retiring in the early 1980s.

Seven

Trains and Boats and Planes (and Buses)

This is one of the earliest paddle steamers to visit Clacton, the *Glen Rosa*, *c.* 1890. Built in 1877 in Scotland, it moved south in 1881 and was put into service on the Thames with the London Steamboat Co. Unfortunately it suffered numerous mechanical problems and the cry '*Glen Rosa* late again' was frequently heard. It was sold to a Bristol firm in 1896 and left the area.

The most famous line to visit Clacton during the late Victorian and Edwardian period was the Belle Steamers. This is the *Clacton Belle*, the first of the line, shortly after its launch in 1890. The competing steamboat companies were well known for racing each other down the Thames. In 1893, as a result of one such race, the master of the *Clacton Belle* was found guilty of reckless navigation and fined. The *Clacton Belle* was scrapped in 1929.

Between the wars, the Eagle Steamers took the place of the Belle Steamers in the popularity stakes. This is the *Crested Eagle* some time in the 1930s. Built in 1925, it was sunk in 1940 helping out at the Dunkirk evacuation.

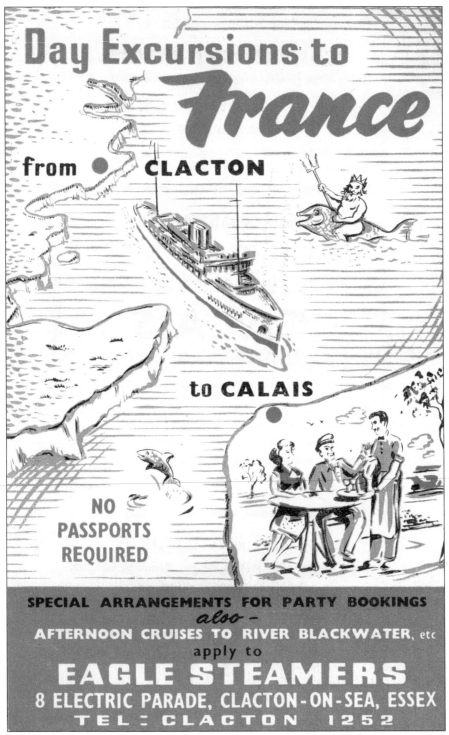

By the 1950s, the shipping trade was in terminal decline. One of the last regular visitors to Clacton was the MV *Queen of the Channel*, which also ran day trips to France as can be seen from this 1958 advertisement. The fare was 40s for adults and 20s for children.

Being on the sea, the lifeboat has played an important part in the life of the town. This is the fifth lifeboat, the *Sir Godfrey Baring*, launched in 1951. It took the full brunt of the 1953 floods and was also called out several times in the early '60s to rescue various pirate radio ships. It was replaced in 1968 by the *Valentine Wyndham-Quinn*, after being called out 226 times, more times than any other Clacton lifeboat.

Jesse Salmon became cox of the lifeboat in 1919 after already having been in the service for thirty-six years and collecting a silver and a bronze medal. After retiring in 1924, he became the official guide at the lifeboat house on the Pier.

Even though the first motor bus to run in Clacton was introduced in 1898, E.M. Appleby continued to run a horse bus service during the Edwardian period and throughout the 1920s under the name Favourite Buses. His stables were in Rosemary Road.

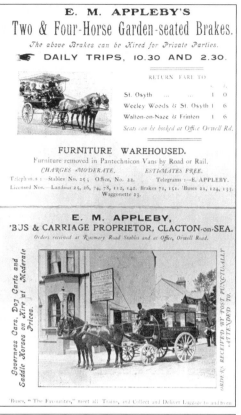

The Silver Queen Omnibus Service was registered in 1913. During the 1920s, when this photograph was taken, it ran services all over the Tendring District. It was eventually acquired by Eastern National in 1932. Their original stand was opposite the old Town Hall.

By 1922 the Silver Queen coach stand had moved to the corner of Hayes Road and Rosemary Road as can be seen in this photograph from that year. There was great competition between Silver Queen and another local company, Enterprise Buses, with drivers and conductors sometimes even fighting over passengers at bus stops!

A novelty advertising postcard produced by the Clacton and District Motor Service Ltd just before the First World War.

The *Swiftsure*'s inaugural run to St Osyth was on 15 August 1906. It was operated by the Clacton-on-Sea Motor Omnibus Co, whose directors were Messrs H. Smith, Bright, Lock and Miller. The *Swiftsure* was used to run excursions to places of interest rather than as a regular bus service.

Charles Barnes established his Progress Coaches business at about the time of the First World War. His first coach, pictured at about that period, was called the Sugar Box because the body was made from sugar packing cases. His first garage was in Warwick Road, but he eventually moved to Pier Avenue, from where the family business continued to operate until its closure in 1987.

Clacton's new railway station, *c.* 1930. The original station was opened in 1882, but was demolished and a new one was built in 1928; the opening ceremony was performed by Mr Whitelaw, Chairman of the London & North Eastern Railway Company, who also took the opportunity to lay the foundation stone for Clacton's new Town Hall at the same time. This was a period of rapid growth and great civic pride in Clacton, as three new major public buildings, the station, Town Hall and County High School, were all opened within a three-year period.

Below opposite: In 1959, the date of this photograph, W.H. Smith still had a bookstall inside Clacton station. On the board to the right of the Vimaltol advert is an announcement concerning the forthcoming electrification of the service to Colchester.

Above: The railway station with an Eastern National bus outside in 1955, a period when public transport was still a more popular means of getting to Clacton than the private car. Summer Saturdays at the station were always very busy.

The first electric train service ran on 13 April 1959; the above photograph shows Sir Reginald Wilson, Chairman of British Railways Eastern Area Board, escorting Captain E.R. Pennell, Chairman of Clacton Urban District Council, to the driving cab at the official opening.

Harold Prescott stands by ready to pilot the Hillman Airways aeroplane from Clacton to Romford, c. 1934. Edward Hillman launched Hillman Airways in 1932 from near his home in Romford; in 1933 he inaugurated a regular service to Clacton which took 45 minutes and cost 25s return.

Eight
Bucket and Spade Time

Clacton beach seen in its infancy some time between 1885, the year the baths were built at the pier head, and 1888, when the sea wall was erected. As yet there are no paths to take holidaymakers down from the cliff top to the beach, just a wooden staircase, and the cliffs themselves are untouched by any man-made landscaping. The bathing machines had arrived on Clacton beach on 1873, owned by James Cattermole and operated by his son Alfred for many years.

In around 1887 a rival bathing machine proprietor in the person of Edmund Almond appeared on Clacton's beach, first on the east beach and later near the Jetty (where Martello Bay is today). The company traded as Finch & Almond. Bathing machines lasted until the First World War, after which a new moral code made them redundant.

By the 1890s, the date of this photograph, an attempt had been made to tidy up the cliff face and the lower promenade had been built.

This crowded Edwardian beach scene from around 1910 shows that even when the tide was in there was still plenty to do. The building on the right was a sea water pumping station built in 1899 to pump water round to standpipes dotted around the town for council workmen to wash down the dusty streets. It was demolished in 1963.

This view from around 1910 shows that not everything happened on the beach immediately next to the Pier. Here crowds are enjoying the archaically named 'Jolly Coons'.

Back on the west beach, next to the Pier, *c.* 1910. The crowds seem to be watching the arrival of the lifeboat, the *Albert Edward*, the third lifeboat to be given the same name. In the foreground is Claude North's 'Living and String Marionettes' stand. His son, Claude North Junior, continued the tradition until well after the Second World War by operating a Punch and Judy show on the same spot.

The east beach has never been as popular as the west beach. Nevertheless, this view from around 1905 shows a certain amount of activity on the beach as well as a small band playing to the holidaymakers. Jack Holland's Concert Party were regular performers on this stretch of beach.

In 1898 a smaller version of the pier was built at the far west end. Called the Jetty and seen here around 1908, it was supposed to have been used for the barges bringing building materials to the new town of Clacton. But it was not used much and became a small pleasure pier between the wars. It was demolished in 1940 as a wartime precaution.

75

The west beach continued in popularity until the 1950s, the date of this photograph. As can be seen there is hardly any room left on the beach, a sign of just how popular Clacton was at this period. The striped kiosk to the left is Claude North Junior's Punch & Judy show and the pleasure boat just arriving is *Nemo II*.

Nine

No. 1 North Sea

The Pier was the first building to be built in the new town of Clacton-on-Sea. Clacton was the brainchild of Peter Bruff who bought up the land with the sole intention of turning it in to a seaside resort. As there was no railway at the time and the roads were no better than cart tracks, he realized the best way of getting visitors to his resort was by sea. When first built in 1871 the Pier was only 300 yards long and 12 feet wide. By the time of this photograph (taken c. 1880) it had already been considerably lengthened.

As can be seen from these early photographs – this one is from 1893 – the Pier was originally built purely as a landing stage. The first recreational use for the Pier came in 1885 when the owner of the Royal Hotel built his hot and cold sea water baths. Then in 1893 a theatre, the Pier Pavilion, was built. This can be seen here under construction.

During the Edwardian period the Pier Pavilion was home to a concert party under the direction of Will Pepper called the 'White Coons'.

During the early years of this century Professor Webb performed stunt dives off the Pier to amuse the crowds. The bicycle dive seen here in 1908 was one of his most famous dives. He lived until he was ninety-five with, it is said, never a day's illness.

Just after the First World War the Pier was bought by Ernest Kingsman, who set about turning the Pier into an amusement and entertainment centre. His first innovations, as can be seen from this photograph from around 1923, were Skeeball and the Blue Lagoon Dance Hall.

By 1936, the date of this photograph, Kingsman had spent hundreds of thousands of pounds on improvements, including a new Blue Lagoon Dance Hall to the right of the entrance, a swimming pool and a new theatre, the Ocean Theatre.

This photograph, taken in 1938, is evidence that Kingsman was continually extending the Pier and building new attractions. By the outbreak of war, Clacton had become the most popular pier in the country in terms of numbers of visitors and also the largest in area.

The Pier Swimming Pool, opened in 1932, was the first open air swimming pool to be built on a pier anywhere in the country. This view is from the 1950s.

Another major Kingsman attraction was the roller coaster known as the Steel Stella, seen here in 1954. It was built in 1937 and destroyed by fire in 1973.

Another 1954 view, this time of the Cresta Run. Kingsman died during the Second World War but his family, notably his son Barney, continued to run the pier until 1971.

The most popular entertainer to perform on the Pier was Clown Bertram, seen here during the 1930s. He entertained children (and their parents) every season from 1922 until 1939. In 1938 he appeared on the radio programme *In Town Tonight*, for which he received a fee of three guineas plus a further 15s 9d for the rights to 'mechanical reproduction to the Empire.'

Bertram started off performing in the open air with the children sitting on mats and the parents in deck chairs at the back, but eventually Kingsman built him his own theatre called the Children's Theatre, seen here around 1930.

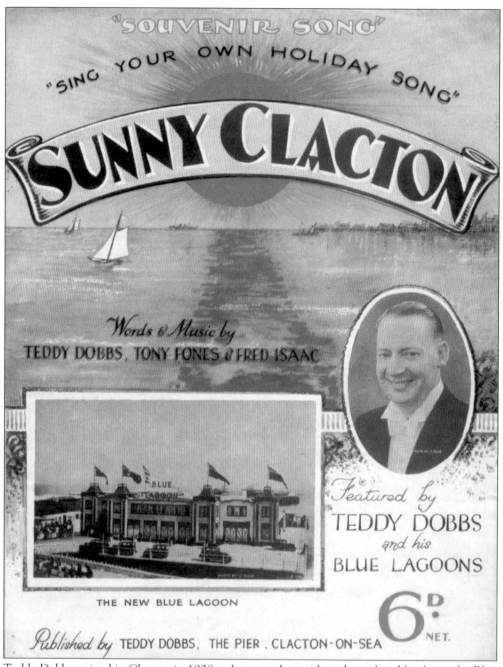

Teddy Dobbs arrived in Clacton in 1928 to become the resident dance band leader at the Blue Lagoon right through to the 1950s. He even wrote a song about Clacton called 'Sunny Clacton'. This is a copy of the sheet music cover, published around 1935.

The Ramblas open air concert party appeared at the end of the Pier from 1932 until 1964. They are seen here in 1961, with their post-war producer and star, Gordon Henson, on the extreme left. Claire Ruane is second from the right.

From 1928 until its closure in 1978 the Ocean Theatre brought many star names to Clacton. Before the war, these included George Robey and Albert Whelan; after the war there were Tony Hancock, Frankie Howerd, Benny Hill and Julie Andrews. This is the Dehl Trio in 1957 with the Ocean Girls.

The 1970s saw more big names including Leslie Crowther (seen here with Johnny Vyvyan and the Karlins at the foot of the Cresta Run in 1971), Dick Emery, Arthur Askey and Russ Abbot, but they weren't enough to prevent the Ocean Theatre's decline in fortunes and eventual closure.

Ten

From Pierrots to
the Pictures

The first concert party to set out its stall in Clacton was probably L'Art Minstrels who arrived in 1892. Popplewell and Pullan's Yorkshire Pierrots arrived on the West Beach in 1901 and performed regularly every summer until 1912, in which year a big wave washed their stand out to sea! In 1905, the approximate date of this photograph, they were paying the Council £4 rent per week in advance, while Claude North was getting away with £2 for his pitch.

Harry Frewin left the Yorkshire Pierrots shortly after their debut to set up his own group, the White Coons, at the far end of the beach. With the arrival of Will Pepper's older established White Coons, Frewin changed the name of his group to the Jolly Coons. This is a picture of them in 1907, though, it must be said, they don't look very jolly...

The concert party which left the longest lasting influence on Clacton was founded by Bert Graham in 1894 as the London Concert Company. By 1899, he had been joined by Bernard Russell and Will Bentley (all three shown here, c. 1908) and after a somewhat peripatetic existence they settled down on a patch of land in Tower Road called the West Cliff Gardens.

Stanley Holloway, pictured here in 1913, was a member of the group from 1912 to 1914, during which time his wages went up from £3 13s 6d per week to £4 14s 6d. He married his first wife Queenie in Clacton. They lived in Beatrice Road and later Ellis Road. After his first appearance in 1912, the local paper reported that he was 'A pleasant baritone who sings the songs that please the audience.'

The old West Cliff Gardens Theatre, seen here around 1905, was made of wood and canvas and the sides could be rolled up on hot summer evenings to let the air in. The present West Cliff Theatre was built on the same site in 1928 and is, of course, still going strong today.

In 1934, Bert Graham and Will Bentley (Bernard Russell had died in 1910) sold the theatre to Will Hammer, the founder of Hammer House of Horror, who continued to put on shows there until his death in 1957. This is the 1935 company consisting of Jack Richards, Winifred Dunk, Walter Newman, Marjorie Holmes, Bernard Brightwell, Maude Merlins, Edward Laing, four dancers and Eric Barker.

The Operetta House, built as part of the Town Hall Buildings in 1894, became a cinema in 1911 and reverted to a theatre after the Second World War. Re-christened the Savoy Theatre, it attracted the very biggest names in show business to Clacton in the 1950s, the date of this photograph, including Max Miller, Alma Cogan and Billy Cotton.

This is Clacton's town band outside Clement Harman's Warehouse in Orwell Road, *c.* 1890. Clement Harman was the son of James Harman, one of Clacton's leading pioneers and father of Sir James Harman, Lord Mayor of London. The band was formed in 1886 under the leadership of George Badger and was contracted by the Council to play for seven hours per day.

In 1899 a bandstand was built on the East Promenade opposite the Royal Hotel for the town band and visiting German bands. This photograph was taken around 1910, at which time the conductor was George Wright, whose favourite tune was *Poet & Peasant*.

Originally band concerts were free, but after a short while the area was fenced off and a 3d admission charge made. This is the staff who collected the money around 1905.

As part of the 'general beautifying programme' when the Venetian Bridge was built, a new fully enclosed band pavilion was also constructed and the bandstand moved into it. In 1936 the bandstand was removed to be replaced by a stage. This shows the building work in process.

The Band Pavilion was used for many forms of entertainment in addition to band concerts. The Daily Mirror 8, shown here in the late 1930s, were regular visitors between 1936 and 1939.

After the war the resident band was Younkman and his Czardas, seen here in 1947. They were followed by Bobby Howell.

But it was Ronnie Mills who became the undoubted star of the Band Pavilion from his arrival in 1953 until he left in the late 1960s. He was tremendously popular and never failed to pack the crowds into the Pavilion. He also hosted shows such as the Ideal Holiday Girl Contest, seen here in the Pavilion in the late 1950s.

The Palace, Clacton-on-Sea.

The Palace-by-the-Sea was opened in 1906, the date of this photograph, and was based on the Earl's Court exhibitions then in vogue. It contained attractions from all round the world, including a Japanese Pagoda and a replica of the Blue Cave of Capri.

The first moving pictures in Clacton were shown at the West Cliff Gardens Theatre in 1898 as a one-off but in 1905 the Operetta House began regular showings of 'Biograph Animated Pictures'. The Bioscope Operator was Mr Gilbert Copley, seen here in 1905. In 1911 The Operetta House was converted into Clacton's first proper cinema.

Clacton's first purpose-built cinema, The Kinema – later the Kinema Grand – was built in 1913 in West Avenue. This photograph dates from just before the First World War. The Kinema Grand was demolished in 1962.

His Majesty

King

George V.

Silver

Jubilee

Celebrations

By kind permission of the Proprietors

AN INVITATION

to the

ELECTRIC CINEMA, Great Clacton, at 10.30 a.m.

on MONDAY, MAY 6th, 1935,

FOR A SPECIAL JUBILEE ENTERTAINMENT.

Great Clacton also had its own cinema, the Electric Theatre, opened in 1922 on the site of the old maltings which had been destroyed in a fire the year before. This is an invitation to a special event held at the cinema in 1935 to mark King George V's Silver Jubilee. The cinema closed on the outbreak of war.

The Odeon in West Avenue, seen here in 1956, was opened on 30 May 1936 with the film *Jack of All Trades* starring Jack Hulbert. It seated 1,214 and was the latest word in comfort. The building was demolished in 1984. It was the fifth of Clacton's six cinemas, the last one being the Century, today's only surviving cinema.

The Carnival was begun in 1922 by Ernest Kingsman as a fundraising event for Clacton Hospital. The most popular part of the Carnival has always been the procession. This is the Oulton Hall entry in the late 1930s.

Radio personality Kenneth Horne is seen inspecting one of the eighty-two coaches which took part in Britain's first ever coach rally in 1955, with entries converging on Clacton from London, Bedford, Cambridge and Norwich. The other two judges pictured are Inspector Priestly and Mrs Ferguson.

The donkeys pictured here in the mid 1950s were part of a long tradition of donkey rides in Clacton; the first operator was licensed in 1886 with the last going out of business in 1997.

Pleasure boats were also a popular pastime for many years. This is the *Gay Commodore* which operated off the Pier in the immediate post-war years.

The 100-seater *Viking Saga*, seen here in the 1950s, was owned by the lifeboat coxswain, Dick Harman, and operated for many years by Len Austin. Its last season in Clacton was 1973.

The *Nemo II* was also owned by Dick Harman for many years, who took it over in the early 1950s, the approximate date of this photograph. It had begun serving Clacton in 1928 and continued until 1982. 1983 was the first year in living memory in which there were no pleasure boats operating off Clacton beach.

Clacton Town Football Club in the 1930s. Clacton Town's first ever match was on 2 December 1892 when they lost 4-1 to Colchester Crusaders. In 1935 they became founder members of the Eastern Counties League, the league they are in today.

They did, however, spend some time in the Southern League in the 1950s and '60s, and this is the team which won the Southern League Division One Shield in 1959/60. They established a new record that season by becoming the only team ever to top the league throughout the entire season.

PRICE 3d.

1947

ESSEX v. LEICESTERSHIRE

Played at THE RECREATION GROUND, VISTA ROAD, CLACTON-ON-SEA
(By kind permission of the Clacton Urban District Council).

SATURDAY, MONDAY AND TUESDAY, AUGUST 9th, 11th AND 12th.

HOURS OF PLAY :—First 2 Days, 12 noon till 7.30 p.m. 3rd Day, 11.30 a.m. till 5 or 5.30
LUNCHEON INTERVAL :—First 2 Days, 2.0 to 2.40 p.m. ; 3rd Day, 1.30 to 2.10 p.m.
TEA INTERVAL.—According to state of game.

Umpires : HENDREN, D. & MILLS, P. T.   * Captain ; x Wicketkeeper.

ESSEX.

	First Innings.		Second Innings.	
1 DODDS, T. C.	c & b Jackson	69	b Jackson c & b Sperry	9
2 CRAY, S. J.	Run out	51	run c Jackson	
3 CRABTREE, H. P.	c Jackson b Walsh	9	c Walsh b Jackson	16
4 VIGAR, F.	st Riddington b Jackson	72	b b c Jackson	48
5 T. E. BAILEY	c Jackson b Walsh	14	not out	68
* 6 T. N. PEARCE	not out	16		
7 D. R. WILCOX	c Walsh	15	b Walsh c Watson	4
8 D. J. INSOLE	b Lester	23	c J. b Jackson	4
9 SMITH, R.	c & b Walsh	9	not out	13
10 SMITH, P.	c b Prentice	24		—
x11 WADE, T. H.	not out	20		—
Extras	... b—, lb—, nb—, w—	—	b—, lb—, nb—, w—	—

TOTAL ... 420 9 dec.   145 for 6

FALL OF WICKETS—First Innings.   Second Innings.

1	2	3	4	5	6	7	8	9	10	1	2	3	4	5	6	7	8	9	10
75	46	174	263	215	215	267	237	405	400	4	12	14	16	80	102				

BOWLING ANALYSIS

	First Innings.					Second Innings.				
	O.	M.	R.	W.	Nb.	Wd.	O.	M.	R.	W.	Nb.	Ws.

LEICESTERSHIRE.

	First Innings.		Second Innings.	
* 1 BERRY, L. G.	c Vigar b R. Smith	165	not out	111
2 RIDDINGTON, A.	c Wade b P. Smith	33	run out	29
3 WATSON, G.	c Bailey b	25	b R. Smith	14
4 TOMPKIN, M.	st Wade b	45	b	22
5 JACKSON, V.	lbw b	23	not out	14
6 PRENTICE, F.	b	52		
7 LESTER, G.	lbw b	9		
8 HOWARD	c Wade b	4		
9 WALSH, J. E.	b	17		
x10 CORRALL, P.	c Insole b R. Smith	22		
11 SPERRY, J.	not out			
Extras	... b—, lb—, nb—, w—	—	b—, lb—, nb—, w—	—

TOTAL ... 388   272 for 3 dec.

FALL OF WICKETS—First Innings.   Second Innings.

1	2	3	4	5	6	7	8	9	10	1	2	3	4	5	6	7	8	9	10
75	111	134	164	299	319	341	343	376	388	34	196	248							

BOWLING ANALYSIS.

	First Innings.					Second Innings.				
	O.	M.	R.	W.	Nb.	W.	O.	M.	R.	W.	Nb.	W.
P. Smith	20	4	68	2	—	—						
R. Smith	55.2	6	98	2	—	—						
Insole	8	0	20	0	—	—						
T. E. Bailey	15	4	41	0	—	—						
Vigar	13	3	111	0	—	—						

Scorers: S. COE and G. ROLFE

Between 1931 and 1966, Essex played county cricket at the Vista Road Recreation Ground
for one week in August. This is the scorecard for the match against Leicestershire played in
1947. In that match, Essex player Ray Smith passed both 1,000 runs and 100 wickets for the
season.

Eleven

Hi-de-Hi!

Billy Butlin opened his first camp in Skegness in 1936 and his second in Clacton in 1938.
When it first opened it catered for 1,000 visitors. This view of the Clacton camp swimming
pool dates from 1939.

Before going into the holiday camp business, Butlin ran a string of amusement parks around the country as well as holding concessions at other amusement parks. As can be seen in this photograph from the early 1930s, one concession he held was on Clacton Pier.

Butlin's Camps revolutionized the British holiday with food and entertainments all laid on for the one single price of admission. Campers were divided into houses and points awarded throughout the week for various games and sports. This is the swimming gala taking place around 1970, by which time the camp had expanded to take 6,000 guests.

The main theatre in the camp was the Gaiety Theatre, seen here in 1970. Before the war it attracted stars such as Elsie and Doris Waters, Vic Oliver and Mantovani, while after the war it starred names such as Arthur Askey, Arthur English and Ted Rogers.

Before the war – this photograph is from 1939 – Butlin's took physical exercise very seriously and held 'drill' every morning. This was often taken by prominent boxers of the time, such as Len Harvey, though clearly not in this case!

The Chef, Butlin's Holiday Camp. *Empire View*

Perhaps you needed physical exercises if you were fed by Joe Velich, the camp chef just before and just after the war. He was everyone's idea of how a chef should look! He could often be seen walking round the dining hall chatting to campers, as well as refereeing boxing matches. Some said he never cooked anything and was just a 'front-of-house' chef.

Radio Butlin's, *c.* 1970. It was from here that campers were bombarded with messages all day about the latest games and forthcoming attractions. It was also Radio Butlin's job to wake up campers at 7.45 each morning to let them know 'It's a lovely day and time for breakfast.'

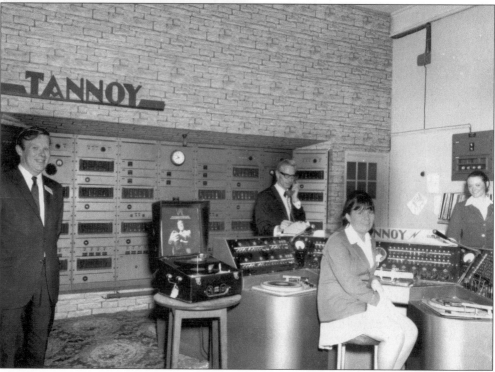

Twelve

Put That Light Out!

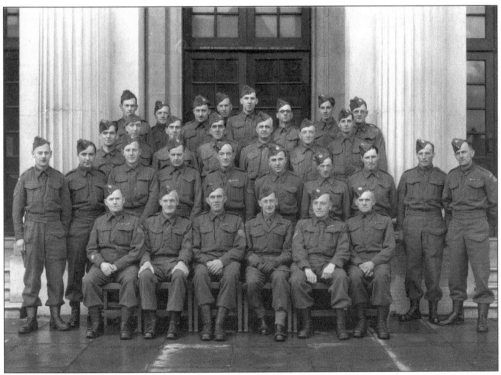

Clacton's own Dad's Army, the Home Guard unit, poses for its photograph outside the Town Hall, *c.* 1941.

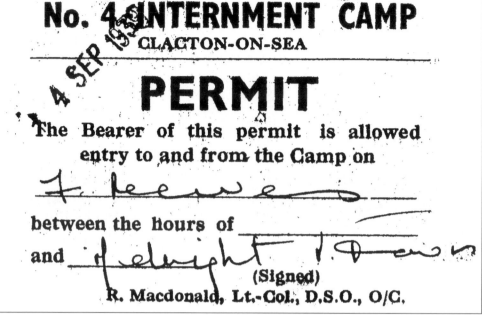

No. 4 INTERNMENT CAMP
CLACTON-ON-SEA

4 SEP 1939

PERMIT

The Bearer of this permit is allowed
entry to and from the Camp on

F. Reeves

between the hours of _____

and _Midnight_ R. ~~~~~~~
(Signed)
R. Macdonald, Lt.-Col., D.S.O., O/C.

When war was proclaimed on 3 September 1939, Butlin's Holiday Camp was taken over by the Government and converted into an internment camp for aliens. Even Butlin's own staff had to be issued with permits if they wished to visit the camp. This one was issued to Frank Reeves on 4 September 1939.

The internment camp did not last very long and Butlin's was very soon taken over by the Army Auxiliary Corps, later the Pioneer Corps. This photograph shows them marching into the camp in 1940.

Emergency supplies were quickly established around Clacton to enable the town to cope with whatever Hitler might throw at it. This is the 5,000-gallon steel drum ARP water tank situated on the corner of Pier Avenue and Hayes Road in 1939.

Five communal air-raid shelters were also established. This one, shown here in 1939, was in the High Street.

This photograph shows the devastation caused in Victoria Road following the explosion of a land mine being carried on a Heinkel bomber which was shot down and crashed just before midnight on 30 April 1940. No. 25 Victoria Road was completely demolished with the occupants, Mr and Mrs Gill, becoming the first civilian fatalities of the war anywhere in mainland Britain.

A second mine was also on board but did not explode. Before it was recognised as such and defused, workers clearing up the rubble had used it as a seat when taking a break. It was eventually loaded on to a Bryan's Garage pick-up truck and taken to Portsmouth for examination.

CLACTON
NAZI RAIDER CRASH!

Every Family is urged to take immediate
advantage of

"JOHN BULL'S"
£200 AIR RAID
INSURANCE
(Underwritten at LLOYDS)

FREE!

FOR EVERY READER

JOHN BULL

EVERY THURSDAY - 2d.

★ *Fill in the Newsagent's*
Order Form on right now
and hand it to your news-
agent as soon as possible.
Fill in the Registration Form
also and post it at once to
"John Bull."

---SIGN TO-DAY---

JOHN BULL

Hand this Form to Your
Newsagent.

To (Name of
Newsagent) ....

Address ....

Please deliver or reserve JOHN BULL
for me weekly until further notice.

Signature ....

Address ....

....

....

Date ....

PLEASE WRITE CLEARLY.
C.G. 3/5/1940

CUT HERE

POST THIS FORM TO
' John Bull.'' Registration Depart-
ment, 128, Long Acre. London W C 2.

I have sent an Order Form to my Newsagent
for the regular weekly delivery of JOHN BULL.
Please register me as a regular reader.

Reader's Signature
Age.............................

Address ....

....

Name and Address
of Newsagent

Use 1d. stamp. Don't seal envelope. A Certificate setting out the full Benefits and Conditions and certifying registration will be sent if
1d. stamped addressed envelope is enclosed for
return.

PLEASE WRITE CLEARLY. C.G. 3/5/1940

Some companies were quick to cash in on what was the first major incident of the war in Britain. This is a leaflet produced by *John Bull* magazine shortly afterwards urging everyone to take out 'air-raid insurance.'

After this incident most of Clacton's schoolchildren were evacuated to the Midlands and West Country. This is St Monica's School in their new surroundings in Chatford, *c.* 1940.

The ATC (Air Training Corps) march down Pier Avenue past the newly opened Anzac Café, *c.* 1942. In the background is the Warwick Castle Hotel, now long since demolished. Now the site is used for Clacton's Saturday market.

Also during 1940, a floating mine badly damaged the Pier. Here Ernest Kingsman is discussing the damage with the 'Man from the Ministry.'

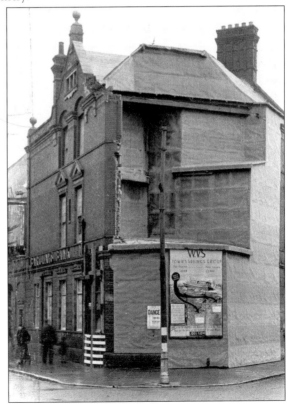

Bombs dropped by a lone raider in May 1941 badly damaged the old Town Hall, and the whole of the front, including the town clock, had to be demolished.

Throughout the war the WVS played a key role in Clacton's wartime activities. The person responsible for running the organization was Lorna Gillespie, seen here in the centre of the back row watching Lady Reading, head of the WVS, greeting Lady Susan Birch on the Town Hall steps in 1945.

VE Day celebrations were held all over Clacton at the end of the war. This is the main victory party taking place at the Brotherhood Hall in 1945. The climax to the celebrations came with a mammoth bonfire on the seafront.

Thirteen
It Happened in Clacton

The end of the First World War was also celebrated with an enormous bonfire on the seafront with an effigy of the Kaiser thrown on top. This is a picture of the peace parade passing the junction of Pier Avenue and West Avenue in November 1918.

In September 1904, large-scale military manoeuvres were held in Essex with Clacton the main landing and re-embarkation point. The officers commandeered Alfred Cattermole's bathing machines as their quarters while the ordinary ranks had to make do with the beach.

This is a picture of the Warwick Castle Hotel and probably dates from 1904, as there is a large number of army officers lined up outside. It is known that many of the senior officers who arrived for the manoeuvres stayed at the Warwick Castle.

Clacton has suffered a number of spectacular fires over the years. This one was at Bromley's Mill in Great Clacton in 1909. It is said that Henry Bromley, the owner, had been in London for the day and as his train approached Clacton he saw a red glow in the sky and wondered what was on fire. He soon found out!

Another Great Clacton fire was this one on 8 August 1921 which destroyed a number of shops, the maltings and a row of old cottages. It was one of the last outings for the old horse-drawn fire engine as it was in 1921 that a decision was made to obtain a new motorized one.

In 1935 a libel action was heard in the High Court in London against the Revd S.M. Morris, Clacton's Baptist minister, for remarks he made in the pulpit about a Sunday concert at the Princes Theatre which were reported in the *Evening Standard*. 'No Sunday Jazz for Clacton' was a float entered in that year's Carnival, reflecting the great amount of interest shown in the case.

The most spectacular fire of them all was the one which started in Lewellen's back yard at about 3 p.m. on Sunday 4 June 1939 and raged for some three hours before being brought under control, although it wasn't until the next morning that it was finally put out.

By the time it was over most of the east side of Pier Avenue from Station Road to Marine Parade had been destroyed. This photograph shows fireman Bernie Howard on top of the turntable ladder trying to douse the flames.

This fire started in the loft of the West Cliff Theatre on 12 July 1950 and destroyed the grid, battens, ropes and pulleys, and much of the scenery, tabs and curtains. The whole town rallied round the rescue operation and just three days later the theatre was ready to re-open. Will Hammer came down to Clacton to thank everyone personally for their support.

PROGRAMME
OF THE PUBLIC
OPENING
OF THE
CLACTON-ON-SEA
COUNTY HIGH
SCHOOL

BY THE RIGHT HON.
LORD RAYLEIGH,
F.R.S.,

on Wednesday, 28th November,
1928, at 3.0 p.m., in the Concert
Hall, at the Band Pavilion.

Clacton County High School opened on 28 November 1928 and was the first of the three major public buildings to open (see p. 68). The programme for the opening consisted of a number of speeches from various dignitaries including the Chairman and Vice Chairman of Governors, Mr George Gardiner and Mrs Florrie Coleman.

When Mr Learoyd became headmaster of St Osyth Road School he encouraged a strong competitive spirit. The school won many awards for football, cricket, netball and hockey and, as can be seen here in this certificate from 1930, even folk dancing.

HM Queen Mary decided to break with tradition in 1938 and instead of going to Balmoral for the summer she planned a series of country visits, including one to Lady Byng at Thorpe Hall in June. During this visit she came to Clacton to inspect a parade of Clacton's ex-servicemen. She is seen here in the company of Brigadier-General Kincaid-Smith of St Osyth Priory.

DATE	EVENT	ORGANISED BY	VENUE	TIME
May 25 – 28	Commonwealth and Empire Exhibition	Toc H, Clacton Branch	Town Hall	3 p.m. daily
31	Religious Service for Children	Clacton Schools	Band Pavilion	9.30 a.m.
31	United Service	Clacton Council of Churches	Town Hall	3 p.m.
June 1	Old People's Tea Party	Clacton Rotary Club	St. James' Hall	2 p.m.
1	Old People's Tea Party	W.V.S.	Great Clacton Women's Institute	
2	Television for Old People	Rotary Club in conjunction with L. Barr and Co.	Town Hall	10 a.m. to 5 p.m.
2	Television for Old People	Clacton Round Table	Private Homes	
2	Television for Residents of Pension Age	Holland-on-Sea Coronation Committee and F. W. Hazelton	Public Hall	10 a.m. to 6 p.m.
2	Television Coronation Programme	L. Barr and Co.	Clacton and District Hospital Dr. Barnardos Homes	
2	Special Coronation Night	Management of	Band Pavilion	7.45 p.m.
2	Special Coronation Night	Management of	Westcliff Theatre	8 p.m.
2	Special Coronation Night	Management of	Savoy Theatre	8 p.m.
2	Coronation Ball and Cabaret	Clacton Pier	Blue Lagoon	8 p.m.
2	Golf Competition	Clacton Golf Club	Clacton Golf Club	
2	Television	Clacton Golf Club	Clacton Golf Club	
2	Flannel Dance	Clacton Golf Club	Clacton Golf Club	8.30 p.m. to 1 a.m.
3	" Merrie England "	Clacton Choral Society	Town Hall	7.45 p.m.
3	Children's Sports	Holland-on-Sea Coronation Committee	Public Hall Grounds	10 a.m.
3	Finals of Children's Sports	Holland-on-Sea Coronation Committee	Public Hall Grounds	2.30 p.m.
3	Baby Show	Holland-on-Sea Coronation Committee and Holland-on-Sea B.R.C.S.	Public Hall	3 p.m.
3	Resident Children's Tea Party	Holland-on-Sea Coronation Committee and Holland-on-Sea Women's Institute	Public Hall	3.30 p.m.
3	Marionettes	Holland-on-Sea Coronation Committee	Public Hall	5.30 p.m.
3	Social	Holland-on-Sea Coronation Committee and Holland-on-Sea Toc H.	Public Hall	7.30-12 p.m.
4	Tea Parties for Residents of Pension Age	Holland-on-Sea Coronation Committee and Holland-on-Sea B.R.C.S.	Public Hall	3, 4 and 5 p.m.
4	Old Tyme Dance	Holland-on-Sea Coronation Committee and Holland-on-Sea Public Hall Social Club	Public Hall	7.30-12 p.m.
6	9th Annual Philatelic Convention	Association of Essex Philatelic Societies	Westcliff Hotel	12.30 to 6 p.m.
10	Coronation Pageant (Elizabeth I to Elizabeth II)	London Road School	London Road School	2.30 p.m.
13	Tea Party	North Ward Ratepayers' Association	Pathfields School	
15 for 6 days aft. and even. Mornings	Full length Technicolour Film "A Queen is Crowned "	Management	Odeon Cinema	
June 15	(Children) "A Queen is Crowned "	Management	Odeon Cinema	10 a.m.
16	(O.A.P.'s) "A Queen is Crowned "	Clacton Urban District Council	Odeon Cinema	" "
17	(Children) "A Queen is Crowned "	Management	Odeon Cinema	" "
18	(O.A.P.'s) "A Queen is Crowned "	Clacton Urban District Council	Odeon Cinema	" "
19	(Children) "A Queen is Crowned "	Management	Odeon Cinema	" "
17	Blind People's Outing	Clacton Blind Club		
18	Tea Party	Red Cross Darby and Joan Club	B.R.C.S. Headquarters, Hayes Road	4.30 p.m.
July 8	Horticultural Show	Clacton District Horticultural Society	Progressive Hall	2.30 p.m.
	Allotments Competition–Coronation Cup Last entry date 30th May 1953	Clacton Urban District Council		

Clacton's celebrations for the Coronation of Elizabeth II in 1953 went on from 25 May right through to 8 July. On 2 June, the day of the Coronation itself, L Barr and Co., electricians, organized a special all-day showing of the Coronation on television at the Town Hall.

121

This photograph shows the coaches ready to leave Clacton Town Hall to take part in BBC TV's *Top Town Tournament*, broadcast on 12 May 1960 from Manchester. Clacton's thirty-six strong team which included Robin Garton, Doreen Bradbrook's Young Ladies, John Emmanuel, Valerie Mills, Billy Houghton, Larry Spencer, Norman Lanry, Roy Williams and Terry Jones, Mary Seymour, Graham Silver, CAOS and, of course, the Young Brothers, Bob and Reg, were unfortunately beaten by St Helier 77 points to 60. Not one to miss a trick, Harry Thompson travelled in front in the Clacton publicity van.

Fourteen
Clacton's Movers and Shakers (and others)

Gordon Jessup, Chairman of Clacton Urban District Council in 1961, is surrounded by that year's Ideal Holiday Girl contestants. Gordon Jessup presented the winner, Jacqueline White of Derby, with her £250 first prize at the Band Pavilion.

Sergeant Abraham Quick in Boer War uniform, *c.* 1899. Sgt Quick raised a unit of men from Clacton to join the City of London Imperial Volunteers. On the morning of their departure they marched to the railway station, led by the Town Band and followed by a large crowd of well-wishers.

Abraham Quick's son, Arnold, not only took over his father's printing and publishing business, but also became a prominent Councillor and a fine cricketer, turning out on occasion for the Essex First XI. At about the time of this photograph, 1950, Quick made the memorable remark that 'Jaywick would not become a garden city overnight.'

Captain E.R. Pennell DFC, of the Royal Flying Corps, pictured here during the First World War, was first elected to Clacton Urban District Council in 1924 and went on to become its chairman in 1927, 1946, 1947 and 1958.

An Edwardian photograph of Clacton's last town crier, 'Peggy' Barnard, showing quite clearly his wooden leg. He owned a shop next to the Plough in Great Clacton. In 1908 he stood for election to the Council and when heckled used to reply, 'Wooden legs are more useful than wooden heads'. He would finish his official announcements with the words, 'God save the King and down with the Liberal Government.'

The staff of Ascham College, *c.* 1916. Ascham College moved to the corner of High Street and Granville Road, Clacton, from Thorpe-le-Soken in 1888. It closed in 1937 and the building was used as ARP Headquarters during the war. It was demolished in 1951 to make way for the telephone exchange which now stands on the site.

Ascham College pupils, photographed in 1920. From left to right, back row: C. Berrill, L. Barr, E. Gray, L. Langdon, H. Canning, R. Folkard. Middle row: H. Paynter, C. Walker, V. West, Mr F.O. Wilson (maths and English teacher), R. Berry, L. Garwood, H. Bates, C. Orrin (football and cricket captain). Front row: R. Hazleton, S. Croydon, B. Bennett, C. Perry, D. Pocock.

The St Osyth Road School football team, *c.* 1930. From left to right, back row: E. Petch, F. Wright, J. Goldsmith (a future chairman of Clacton Urban District Council), B. Whybrow, F. Carter. Middle row: J. Fosker, Mr H. Learoyd (Headmaster), D. Frazer (captain), Mr D.A. Strak, L. Perkins. Front row: S. Gardiner, A. Talbot, B. Curtis.

John Groom's orphanage and crippleage opened in Clacton on 15 July 1889. By the time of this photograph (*c.* 1905) ten houses had been built and accommodation for 240 provided. The orphanage closed when the children were evacuated during the war and was re-opened as a Dr Barnardo's home in 1947. In 1984 all the buildings were demolished.

One of Clacton's great characters was Charlie Wheeler, seen here at the Warwick Castle site in the 1980s. No-one knows where he came from; he just seemed to materialize in the 1920s. After his caravan caught fire in the 1930s he lived rough. During the 1950s and '60s he ran a carousel on the beach at Jaywick. He died in the late 1980s.

Charlie's great friend was this man, 'One-Arm Pip' Page, seen here in 1976. He was born in 1898 and was called up during the First World War. Pip had other ideas and one night he placed his fingers on the railway line just as a train was coming, hoping just to lose the tips and therefore making him ineligible for call-up. Unfortunately the train sliced off most of his arm. Pip died in 1977, having spent most of the previous fifty years living out rough with Charlie Wheeler.